Sniffles, Sneezes, Hiccups, and Coughs

FIRST EDITION
Series Editor Deborah Lock; **Managing Art Editor** Clare Shedden; **US Editor** Elizabeth Hester;
Senior DTP Designer Almudena Díaz; **Production** Allison Lenane; **Picture Researcher** Marie Ortu;
Jacket Designer Katy Wall; **Reading Consultant** Linda Gambrell, PhD

THIS EDITION
Editorial Management by Oriel Square
Produced for DK by WonderLab Group LLC
Jennifer Emmett, Erica Green, Kate Hale, *Founders*

Editors Grace Hill Smith, Libby Romero, Michaela Weglinski;
Photography Editors Kelley Miller, Annette Kiesow, Nicole DiMella; **Managing Editor** Rachel Houghton;
Designers Project Design Company; **Researcher** Michelle Harris; **Copy Editor** Lori Merritt;
Indexer Connie Binder; **Proofreader** Larry Shea; **Reading Specialist** Dr. Jennifer Albro;
Curriculum Specialist Elaine Larson

Published in the United States by DK Publishing
1745 Broadway, 20th Floor, New York, NY 10019

Copyright © 2023 Dorling Kindersley Limited
DK, a Division of Penguin Random House LLC
23 24 25 26 27 10 9 8 7 6 5 4 3 2 1
001–333460–Apr/2023

A catalog record for this book
is available from the Library of Congress.
HC ISBN: 978-0-7440-6814-6
PB ISBN: 978-0-7440-6815-3

DK books are available at special discounts when purchased
in bulk for sales promotions, premiums, fundraising, or
educational use. For details, contact: DK Publishing Special Markets,
1745 Broadway, 20th Floor, New York, NY 10019
SpecialSales@dk.com

Printed and bound in China

For the curious
www.dk.com

Sniffles, Sneezes, Hiccups, and Coughs

Penny Durant

Contents

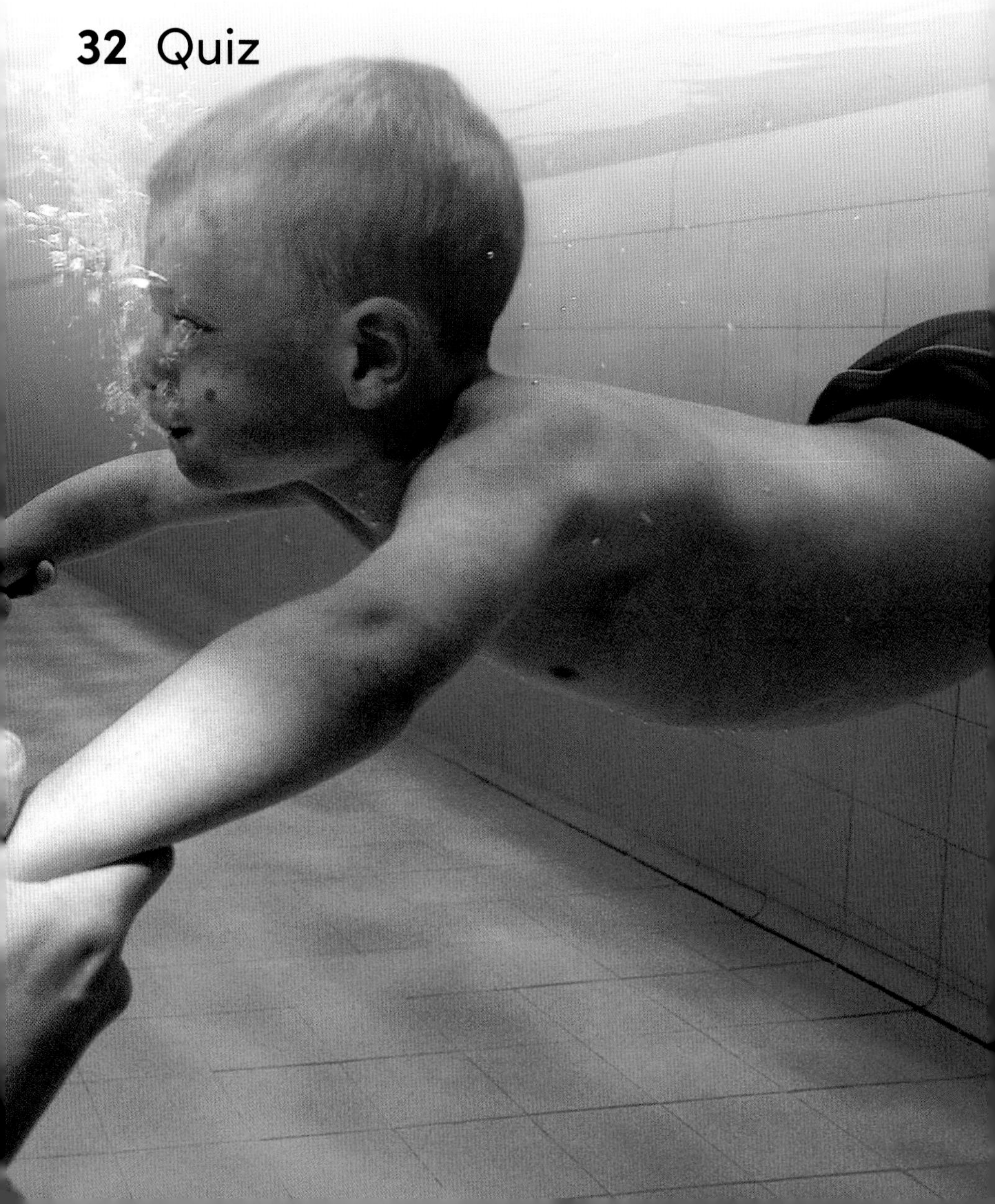

Air and Your Body

Ahhhh...

Ah-choo!
Everyone sneezes—people,
dogs, cats, horses, turtles,
birds, and even giraffes!
Some sneezes are loud.
Others are quiet.

...choo!

Some people sneeze again
and again.
But why do we all sneeze?
And why do we cough,
hiccup, and yawn, too?

You breathe to take in the air
your body needs.
Your nose and mouth are both
passageways for air to get into
your body.
The air travels past your throat
and into the airways
that lead to your lungs.

Diaphragm
This muscle is springy
like a trampoline.
It pulls down and
pushes up as you
breathe in and out.

Your diaphragm [DIE-ah-FRAM],
chest muscles, and brain work
together to keep air going in
and out of your lungs.

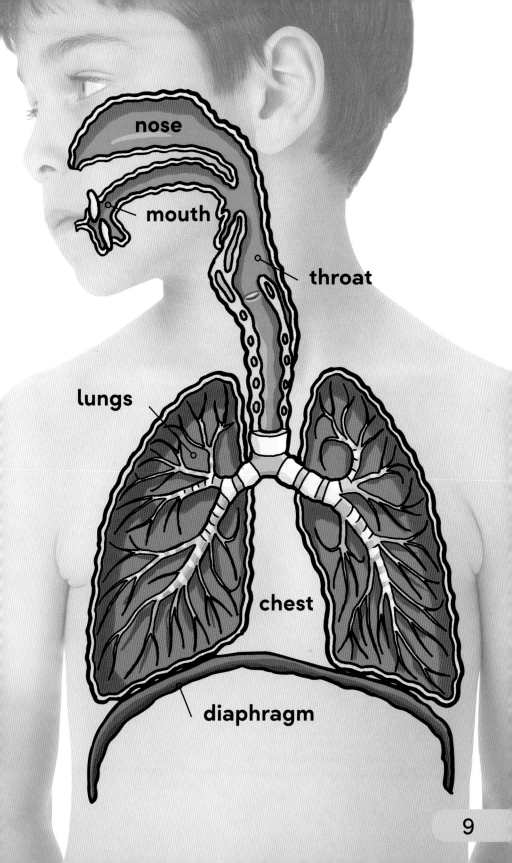

nose

mouth

throat

lungs

chest

diaphragm

Sneezes

The airways to your lungs need to be kept clear all the time.

When you breathe in through your nose, your tiny nose hairs filter the air, and the sticky mucus (snot) collects anything that could be harmful.
It might be dust or pepper or pollen.

House Dust
A speck of dust is not just dirt but a mixture of different things, such as skin flakes, hair, food crumbs, and dust mites.

You feel a tickle.
Your body does not want these things in your nose.
You get the sniffles.
Your brain tells your body to sneeze.

You sneeze more often when you have a cold.
Germs collect in your nose and make it tickle and swell.

Sneezing gets rid of the germs, but they can be spread to other people this way. Sneezing into a tissue stops the germs from spreading.

Some people sneeze when they go out into sunlight.
No one knows why.

Your sneeze could be traveling
at a speed of 100 miles (161 km)
per hour!
The gush of air blows the dust
or germs—and the tickle—
out of your nose.

But what happens if the pollen,
dust, or germs get caught in
your throat or in the airways
to your lungs?
Then, a message is sent
to your brain to tell
your body to cough.

Water droplets,
mucus, dust, and
germs are forced
out of your nose.

Under Pressure

A sneeze travels as fast as a speeding car, so never try to stop it by pinching your nose closed. The pressure can injure your ears.

Coughs

When you have a cold,
you may feel stuffed up
with phlegm [FLEM].

Phlegm is thick, sticky mucus.
It picks up the germs
that have reached your lungs
and airways.
The phlegm needs to be
cleared out so you can
breathe better.
This is why you cough.

Invaders
Germs are tiny living things that
can cause diseases. If they
get into your body, they can
make you sick.

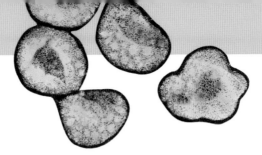

Remember to cover your mouth with your hand when you cough to stop the germs from spreading to someone else.

When you cough, you take a deep breath and hold it, while your chest and stomach muscles tighten.

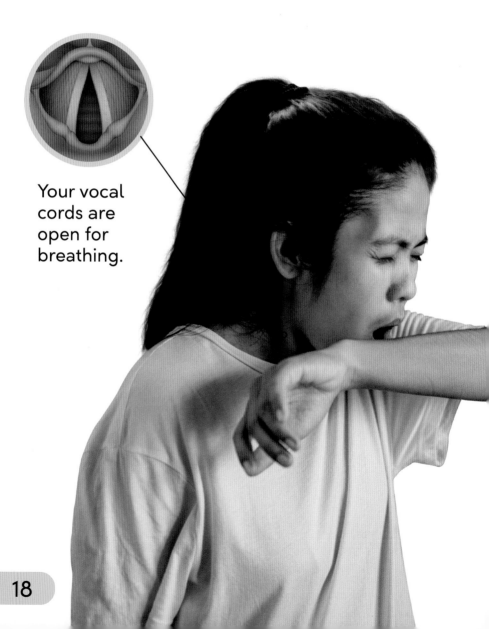

Your vocal cords are open for breathing.

Then, your diaphragm pushes
the air out of your lungs.
The sudden gust of air carries
the pollen, dust, or phlegm
out of your mouth.

As the air rushes over your open
vocal cords, they vibrate and
make a sound.
Your cough might
sound like a
dog barking.

Hiccups

Hic
Hic
Hic

Voice Box
When you want to talk, your breath moves over closed vocal cords, which vibrate to make sounds.

You've got the hiccups.
This may happen if you drink drinks with bubbles or you eat too quickly.

Your diaphragm tightens
in a jerky way.
It pulls in sharply, and you take a quick gulp of air.

Your vocal cords are closed.
They are not ready for the breath that just came in.
When the air hits them,
they make the hiccup sound.

You hiccupped even before you were born.

No one knows why we hiccup, but people try lots of different things to get rid of them. Some people hold their breath. Some breathe in and out of a paper bag.

A paper bag can help you control your breathing.

Some people bend
over and drink
water upside down.

Some people drink water.
Some put sugar on
their tongue.
Some people think
if you are scared or startled,
you will stop hiccupping.

Yawns

If I yawn, will you yawn?
Probably.
Just thinking about yawning
can make you yawn.
When you yawn,
you open
your mouth
very wide.

Huge Yawns

Hippopotamuses have the largest mouth of all land animals. They can open their jaws up to 4 feet (1.2 m) wide.

Your jaw opens and stretches your face and neck muscles. You might close your eyes. You take in a deep breath to fill your lungs. Then, you let it out.

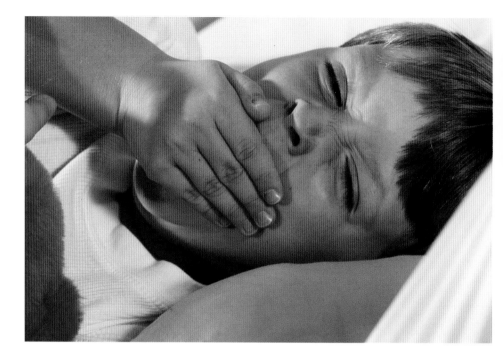

Why do you yawn?
You yawn when you are sleepy
but also when you wake up.

You might yawn if you
are bored but also
when you are not.
Maybe it is your
body's way of saying,
"Let's do something different."

Warm-up Exercise
Athletes yawn before a race. Musicians yawn before a concert. Yawning and stretching make us alert and ready for something new.

Oxygen at Work

Oxygen is in the air that you breathe.
Your whole body needs oxygen to change the food you eat into energy.

In your lungs, oxygen enters your bloodstream and then travels around your body to where it is needed.

Breathing Out
The air you breathe out has carbon dioxide that your body does not need. Plants use carbon dioxide to make their food.

Your body is a marvelous machine!

Glossary

Carbon dioxide
A gas that your body breathes out

Diaphragm
A muscle that moves as you
breathe in and out

Germs
Tiny living things that can cause
diseases

Lungs
Organs, or body parts, that are
used for breathing

Mucus
A sticky material that protects the
body, such as the inside of the nose

Oxygen
A gas in the air that we breathe

Phlegm
A thick, sticky mucus

Pollen
A powder produced by certain
plants

Index

Quiz

Answer the questions to see what you have learned. Check your answers in the key below.

1. When do you sneeze more often?

2. True or False: A sneeze travels slowly.

3. Why should you cover your mouth when you cough?

4. Which part of your body pushes the air out of your lungs?

5. True or False: There is just one way to try to get rid of hiccups.

1. When you have a cold 2. False
3. To stop germs from spreading 4. Diaphragm 5. False